Merry Christmas from

Allen, to

George Pitt

Christmas

1917

The First Church's Christmas Barrel

See page 50.

"'HE THAT HATH PITY UPON THE POOR LENDETH UNTO
THE LORD.'"

THE FIRST CHURCH'S CHRISTMAS BARREL

BY

CAROLINE ABBOT STANLEY

AUTHOR OF "A MODERN MADONNA,"
"ORDER No. 11," ETC.

ILLUSTRATIONS BY
GAYLE PORTER HOSKINS

NEW YORK
THOMAS Y. CROWELL COMPANY
PUBLISHERS

Illustrations

[5]

The First Church's Christmas Barrel

The First Church's Christmas Barrel

I

THOSE who like a "white Christmas" should see one out on the Western plains, where old Mother Earth lies down for her winter sleep under a coverlet so white that from horizon to horizon there is hardly enough gray to outline her form. The winds play tricks with her in scandalous style out there, making roundness where no roundness is and doing their best to lay bare her very bones. "These winds don't care a cuss fer clothes," said Job Tolaver, the stage driver, once; and John Haloran on his hard missionary rides had thought of it a thousand times since. He was saying it to himself numbly now as with stiffening fingers and head lowered against the gale he drove along the faint track of a road.

His wife threw open the door as he drove up, and a stream of light fell athwart the wagon. There was a barrel in the back.

"Dead, John?—or only half?" Her eager eyes searched his face. She knew the whole pitiful story without a word. The draft had not come. Then, because she knew, she went on gayly, "Or have you gone to peddling? What's in your barrel?"

"I don't know yet," he said heavily,

"'DEAD, JOHN?—OR ONLY HALF?'"

twisting it into the room. "We'll see when I've fed Daisy."

When he was gone she eyed the barrel curiously, tilting it and reading aloud:

'REV. JOHN F. HALORAN,
'BLUE LICK, WYOMING.

"It's not potatoes. It isn't heavy enough for that." Then she struck an attitude with clasped hands. "I never saw one before—never! But my prophetic soul tells me this is a missionary barrel. And just two days before Christmas! Well, in the language of my first-born, 'Hooray!'"

When the minister came in there was a comfortable old coat warmed and waiting for him, and a smoking supper set out on a little table drawn up before the stove.

"Sit down, John. I am going to let you eat here in peace away from the children." He glanced up questioningly as a roar came from the kitchen, with snarls and growls in various keys. "It's all right. They are wild animals in a cage and I am the keeper. They are having no end of fun. You had a cold drive."

"Bitter."

"You need an ulster with a storm collar." She glanced involuntarily at the barrel. "Aren't these potatoes good, John? So mealy one hardly needs butter. Lucky thing, too! You didn't know I skimped the family out of a pound of butter, did you? Yes, sir, it went into the candy money." She meant it as a pleasantry, but somehow it failed, and she hurried on. "I wish there were more of the potatoes. Those boys do eat so! But never mind! After Christmas the hens will begin. Funny how hens can tell the time of the year, isn't it?" She chattered on about anything and everything except the draft.

"This certainly is comfort," he said at last, relaxing under the genial influence of food and warmth and companionship. "That's a cold stretch coming out from town."

"Didn't you stop anywhere?"

"Yes. At Joe Henderson's. Mary —his wife died!"

"John!"

"Yes. Died last night. I never felt so sorry for anybody in my life. They think the baby will live; and the poor fellow doesn't know what to do with it nor where to turn."

"Oh, John! If only our cow weren't going dry I would——"

"You shouldn't do it, anyway," he said savagely. "You have enough care now for three women!—Mary, the draft didn't come."

"I know," she said quietly. "But, John, we'll get along some way. It can't last forever. The draft may come next week. And I was joking about the potatoes. We've a lot left."

"It isn't just the money," he said, shaking his head despondently; "it's

the feeling of aloneness in the work.
If I felt that the church back of us
was doing all it could, it would not
be so hard—this 'hope deferred that
maketh the heart sick.' But some-
times I think—they don't care."

"They do, John—they do! Don't
allow yourself to think that. Why,
look at this barrel! I know this is
from some missionary society, and
would any church send us this unless
they knew about our work and were
thinking of us? Why, of course not!
Tell me about the barrel."

"Well, I went to the post-office the
first thing to get the draft. I found
instead a letter from this First Church,
saying they had sent us a barrel. I
went over to the freight office and

there it was. I didn't have enough—"

"How providential that it came before Christmas!" she interrupted. "I'm crazy to see what's in it! Aren't you?"

He did not answer the question directly, being far from feeling her jubilance about it. "We'll open it after a while," he said evasively. In his heart he was protesting, "No! I don't want their barrel! I want my money!"

"But not until the children are off. There will be Christmas things in it that they mustn't see. . . . You got the candy, John? But of course you did."

Her question was unanswered, but she did not notice it.

CHRISTMAS BARREL

"Now I really think the animals will have to come in," she said gayly. "You can be trainer for an hour while this keeper clears up the dishes."

And with a whoop they were upon him—lion, tiger, kangaroo, and baby bear.

When the children were asleep they brought out the barrel—"our charity box," the minister called it, half bitterly.

"I can't help it, John. It may show an impoverished state of the blood—or of the spirit, I don't know which—but when I think of all the things these children need I am glad of this box. I *am*—'charity' though you call it! I am almost sorry you spent the money for candy, for of course there will be a lot of it in here. Well, they will have enough for once in their lives! And they are so starved for candy."

Again he started to speak, but she swept on in full tide of happy talk:

"Before we open it I want to show you the things I already have for them. Of course they will be poor by comparison, so I'll exhibit them first. This overcoat is Paul's, made out of that old, old one of yours with the plaid flannel lining. I turned the fuzzy side out. He thinks it's fine. And with a new one for Paul every overcoat in the line drops a peg and lands on the next younger—so everybody has a change! Then, from the pieces of plaid flannel left I made three good mufflers to tie over their little headies when they scud across the prairies to school. . . . And here are three pairs of mittens cut from the scraps of the coat. I am so proud of myself over those mittens! I had enough yarn to knit Davie's, but——"

"There isn't one woman in a hundred that could have managed so well."

She snuggled up to him. "That pays me—if I needed pay, which I don't. It was a work of love and—well, maybe a little necessity. You told me once that I had a genius for poverty."

"And God knows it has had no chance to lie dormant," he said bitterly.   [19]

"I don't want it to lie dormant. I want every power I possess brought out to the utmost. I truly have enjoyed concocting these things out of nothing. There's nothing that makes a woman feel so virtuous, unless it is getting off a lot of neglected letters. . . . Oh, yes, here are their handkerchiefs—lovely ones made from an old petticoat! But it will make one thing more for the stockings. Isn't it glorious that no matter how much or how little children have at Christmas, they enjoy it just the same? That is, if they have candy. That is the one indispensable. . . . And here are the scrapbooks. I've been saving pictures all year; the blank pages are for 'our special artist'—that's you. I wish I had some colored crayons. Oh, they would love colored crayons! And just think!—only ten cents!"

She was sorry the moment she said it, for a shadow fell upon his face.

"But never mind, John," she said quickly. "Life isn't made up of pinks and greens, and neither is happiness. You can have a whole lot of happiness in this world in gray—if you only know how; and I'm going to teach these children the secret. Now look at my eatables. It is great fun to make a cookie menagerie with one cutter, and that a rabbit. You see, I stick on a trunk, pull down his ears, round him up a bit, and behold an elephant! Then when I want a camel I give Br'er Rabbit two humps, stretch out his jaws, give him a jab almost anywhere—and there's your camel! And look at my dachshund. I laughed till I cried over that. Poor Davie was *so* distressed when I stretched him out.

"And here's a nice red apple for each one. Poor Mary Henderson gave them to me the last time I was over there and I've been saving them ever since. They are a little specked, but I think they will hold out. I did want the oranges, but . . . no, of course you couldn't when the draft didn't come. Anyway, with the candy they won't miss other things. I have the bags all ready—red tarlatan from a peach basket—see?

"There's just one thing I can't get around. I do want something to give the house a Christmas look. I miss that. And there's not a thing here but sagebrush. At home, in Maryland, we had such quantities of holly; and we always made wreaths for the windows and had mistletoe for the chandeliers, and a roaring fire in the open fireplace, and—I can see those parlors now. Those are the memories that cling to us always, I think. I am so sorry that our children can never have them. I hate to think of their lives being utterly devoid of beauty. The East has more than its share."

She was talking more to herself than to him, being momentarily carried off her feet, so to speak, by the flood of recollection sweeping over her of the old home with its mighty oaks, its giant elms, and the hills beyond where Christmas trees could be had for the cutting. The sight of his face brought her back to the present.

"But fortunately Christmas is not dependent upon holly and mistletoe," she said brightly. "They are only the 'outward, visible sign.' We will garnish our home with love and good cheer and contentment. After all, they are the 'inward, spiritual grace.'"

She threw up her head with a gesture habitual to her as if defying fate and its limitations, and his eyes followed her as she moved about the room putting things to rights. What a glorious creature she was!—accepting poverty and bareness as her portion and yet rising above them regally; throwing herself into his work, her own round of toil, her children's pleasures, the neighborhood sorrows—all with the same exuberance of interest and prodigality of self! What would he have been in his work without her, his "missionary coadjutor," as he called her? She was so overflowing with vitality, so undaunted, so alive! A thrill passed through him at the word *alive*. . . . Poor Joe Henderson! Suppose— He covered his eyes and his lips moved.

She was on her knees beside him in an instant.

"John, what is it? What are you saying?"

He took her face between his hands and looked into her eyes. "I was saying: 'Bless the Lord, O my soul; and forget not all His benefits.' "

"I knew you would come to it, John. Now let's open the barrel."

The first thing to come out was a woman's hat-box—a generous one. For years Mary Haloran had worn a small brown felt, trimmed modestly (as became a missionary's wife) with two quills and a knot of velvet. The quills were placed at varying angles from year to year, and the velvet was steamed annually. When it got past that it was placed under the family iron and "mirrored." It always looked respectable, but when Mrs. Haloran saw that spacious box, a swift vision of a black velvet hat with black plumes and a jet buckle—all new at the same time—rose before her.

"I am glad the first thing is for you," John Haloran said. "You deserve it."

They laughed at her efforts to untie it; her fingers were clumsy in her excitement. But it was open at last. She held up to view an old white Leghorn covered with faded flowers. For one moment neither of them spoke. Then her sense of humor came to the rescue and she burst into hysterical laughter.

Putting on the hat she bowed low. "The Reverend Mrs. Haloran, missionary coadjutor! Well, let's see if we can't find something to go with it!"

She found it. And again her ringing laughter pealed out while the minister stood by, the embodiment of outraged dignity. To him there was nothing amusing in this sight. Somebody has said that "for taking us over a trying place a sense of humor is better than the grace of God." Humor was but rudimentary in John Haloran at best, and to-day it was absolutely lacking.

"It is an outrage!" he said.

"It *is* an outrage, John. I grant it. But it's funny!"

It is not our purpose to give here the contents of that barrel. It is sufficient to say that after the first few garments hope died.

"That is all," said Mrs. Haloran at

"AN OLD WHITE LEGHORN COVERED WITH FADED FLOWERS."

last. "No, here is a dear little suit, just right for Davie. And, John, read this note: 'It was my little boy's that is gone.'" Her overwrought nerves gave way then. "Oh, John," she cried, her head on his breast, his arms around her, "we have Davie, anyway, if we haven't the clothes for him. Poor, poor mother!"

A moment later she was putting the garments back.

"It is a disappointment," she said, "but we certainly will not let it spoil our Christmas. We are no worse off, at any rate, than we were before. The things I have will insure the children's good time. The candy alone would do that. . . . John, get me the candy! I'm going to fill the bags now

—to take away the bad taste of this barrel."

The moment which John Haloran had been dreading was upon him.

"Mary, I didn't get the candy."

"Didn't get it?" she echoed blankly.

"No. I used the money to finish paying freight on this barrel."

"John Haloran! You *didn't!*"

"There was no other way. I hadn't enough without."

"The children's candy money!" she said slowly. "Money that I have been hoarding up, five cents at a time, for months! . . . Why, John, Davie has been praying for candy!"

"What could I do, Mary? They wouldn't let me have it at the freight office without the money. I barely

had enough as it was. And I supposed, of course, there would be things
in it for the children—never dreamed
of anything else."

"For fifty cents," she said as if to
herself, not heeding him, "they could
have got enough candy to satisfy
these children—and they didn't do it!
And for one dollar they could have
given them a Christmas that they
would never have forgotten. They
could! One dollar at the ten-cent
store would have got them a book and
a toy apiece, and two pounds of ten
cent candy. And our children would
have thought that was a glorious
Christmas—poor little tads!"

She had been speaking slowly and
in a low voice. Now she said with

sudden anger: "I know the kind of women that sent these things. They are the kind that go up and down fashionable city streets saying to every acquaintance they meet: 'Do tell me what to get for my boy! He has everything in the world you can think of now!' . . . And I would be satisfied with one dollar for my four! Then after Christmas they groan: 'What *shall* I do with all these things?' . . . And I would be glad to pick up after mine all Christmas week if they only had something to throw around! There's nothing right nor fair about it! Now!"

This mood was so new to her that her husband was speechless before it.

"Well! this barrel is going back to

them—to-morrow. To think of their expecting us to pay freight on the wretched thing!"

"Mary! You wouldn't do that!"

"I would—and shall! I'm going to give these people one lesson in giving that they won't forget! A Christmas box for a lot of children out on the plains and no candy in it! And Davie praying for candy! . . . Well! he's going to have it. I'll take this barrel back to town to-morrow myself; and when I come back I shall have the candy."

"Wife, you know I would be only too glad to give you the money if I had it. But I have only two cents left in my pocket until the draft comes! . . . Are you going to ask credit?"

Asking credit was the one humiliation they had spared themselves.

"No. I am going to pay money for it—good money—but I am going to have it!"

In all their life together he had never seen her like this. He watched her with fascinated eyes. Going to the mantel, she took down a box with a slit in the top. It was their missionary bank and was held as sacred from profaning touch as the ark of the Lord. She was tearing it open.

"Mary!" he cried, aghast. "Not the missionary money! You wouldn't take that! 'Will a man rob God?'"

"I'd rob anybody!" she said, turning upon him like a lioness defending her young. "I'm going to have a

CHRISTMAS BARREL

Christmas for my children with candy in it if the heathen go—to perdition!"

He saw then that she was past talking to.

II

IT was about two weeks after this
that the pastor of the First
Church called a meeting of the
ladies of the congregation to take action about a missionary box.

"Another!" groaned several ladies
who never contributed.

He went on to explain that a barrel
sent from the church a few weeks before had been returned, and then—not
scorning to make appeal to any God-
given attribute of the female mind—
added: "Perhaps I should say that this
barrel has been not only returned but
refused. Since it was sent from the

church it is a matter in which you are all interested. The president of the Missionary Society requests a full attendance."

Naturally she got it. Seldom in the annals of the First Church had there been such a meeting.

Ladies,"—the president's tap broke upon a lively hum,—"we are called upon to face a most unprecedented state of affairs. As the meeting to-day is so much larger than the usual attendance at our Missionary Society—so very much in excess of the one that launched this enterprise"—there was marked irony in the implication—"I feel called upon to explain. At our October meeting it was decided to send a box to a poor minister's family in the West, and you were all urged to contribute as liberally as possible. You will remember that the call was one given from the pulpit to the entire church. How you responded to that call we shall soon see."

There was a startled movement, quickly controlled, in several quarters.

"I was called from the city in November and placed the packing of the box in the hands of another."

There was a slight stir in the second row, but Mrs. McArthur raised a protesting hand.

"One moment, please. The barrel was sent out as a Christmas offering from the First Church—not the Missionary Society, mind you, but our wealthy First Church. It was returned immediately. With it came this letter, which I will now read, since it concerns you all."

The president of the Missionary Society was generously sharing honors with the church.

"This is from the wife of the missionary to whom the box was sent—Mrs. Mary C. Haloran. I do not know Mrs. Haloran personally, but I am told by a lady of this congregation at whose suggestion the box was sent that she is a cultivated Christian *lady*. They have a family of four boys, ranging in age from five to eleven. This I ascertained definitely, in order that there might be no haphazard, misfit giving. I left that paper with one of our members."

She looked the assemblage over interrogatively and a lady rose with evident reluctance.

"Madam President—I am ashamed to acknowledge it, but that paper was never sent to the Society. I simply forgot it."

The president shook her head sadly. "It has placed us in a mortifying position. I am sure Mrs. Woodley will pardon me for saying that it exemplifies the truth of the old saying:

"Evil is wrought by want of thought
As well as by want of heart."

Mrs. Woodley sat down with a very red face.

"The evil in this case you will see from Mrs. Haloran's letter, which I will now read:

THE FIRST CHURCH'S

"DEAR MADAM:

"The barrel so generously sent by the First Church is received and its contents are carefully noted. I find after prayerful consideration of our wardrobes that we really are not in need of the articles contained in it, and I return it thus promptly that it may be used in discharging the obligations of the First Church to some of its other missionaries. If sent to the right place—say to a self-respecting minister with a wife whose spirit has not been entirely crushed out by the burdens of frontier life—I should think it might be used several times for this purpose.

"I add a small contribution in the shape of Scripture texts, which will enhance the value of your gifts. The home missionary is so accustomed to subsisting on the Word of God that he may be able to feed on these and be filled. Likewise, they may have the effect to clothe him with the garment of praise. It is perhaps not too much to hope that they may also do good (incidentally) to them that are of the household of faith in the First Church. To this end I will ask that they be read to the ladies of your Society while an inventory of the barrel is taken.

"Very sincerely yours,

"MARY C. HALORAN."

"That's a spicy letter," whispered one woman to another with a sparkle of appreciation. "The woman's no fool—if she *did* go into Home Mission work."

"Madam President," said one a little more obtuse, "that is a very singular communication. It doesn't tell us at all why the barrel was returned."

"The barrel will explain itself," returned the president, grimly, "and will also interpret the letter. We will do exactly as Mrs. Haloran requests —take an inventory and listen to the Scripture messages. The secretary will read."

Then a most unprecedented thing (for a Missionary meeting) occurred. The ladies in the back part of the room came forward.

The president drew from the barrel the same promising hat-box that we have seen, and the women craned their necks. Black velvet and plumes flitted through their brains too, as for one blissful moment they had through the mind of the woman on the plains. Mrs. McArthur handed a slip of paper to her assistant and held up to the astonished gaze of her audience—the old Leghorn.

"'God loveth a cheerful giver,'" read Mrs. Wellman.

There was a burst of laughter in which the donor joined—but with dry lips.

A second box was drawn forth. It elicited another laugh, somewhat less spontaneous than the first, for it was a child's summer hat trimmed with forget-me-nots.

" 'He that hath pity upon the poor lendeth unto the Lord,' " read Mrs. Wellman, adding sarcastically: "How many loans the Lord needs, ladies, of this particular variety, I don't know. Not many, I should think."

"There are others," said the president, unconsciously lapsing into slang, and holding up in each hand a man's dust-grimed straw hat. The secretary read tellingly:

" 'And the Levite that is within thy gates; thou shalt not forsake him.' "

There were those who could not resist the grim satire of this, but more faces were indignant than smiling now, and whispers of, "Who on earth sent those things?" passed from one to another.

"Sh!" said one. "Look at that, will you?"

It was a relic of the past, a faded pink cloth opera cloak with a border of moth-eaten swan's-down which sent out over them a feathery cloud at the president's deft manipulation.

" 'Lay up for yourselves treasures in Heaven,' " read Mrs. Wellman, when the coughing incident to floating down had subsided, " 'where neither moth nor rust doth corrupt, and where thieves do not break through nor steal.' "

They laughed. It was not in unsanctified human nature not to laugh at that. But a seal-clad woman in the fourth row, with a face aflame, looked neither to right nor left, but straight at the garment. She had thought when she sent it in: "It is a nice piece of cloth, anyway, and people like that always know how to dye things. Or she can use it for a baby cloak." It seemed monstrous to' her now.

"Madam President," said an indignant voice, "is there nothing in that barrel fit to wear?"

The president held up two beautiful little winter dresses. "Yes. There are these. And some really nice baby clothes—for Mrs. Haloran's boys! The need of a missionary census, ladies, before sending out a box is self-evident."

She looked in the direction of the recreant Mrs. Woodley, who murmured, " 'Whereas I was blind, now I see!' "

"The next is a contribution to the minister himself." She handed a paper to Mrs. Wellman, who read:

" 'If there be a poor man of one of thy brethren . . . thou shalt open thine hand wide unto him and shalt surely lend him sufficient for his need.' "

"It ought to be a whole suit for that," came a stage whisper. The president held up the offering which was to be sufficient for the poor man's needs. It was a vest!

"Old vests!" came an outraged protest.

There was a disposition to lapse into mirth when another vest was elevated, but it died away as Malachi's burning words fell upon their unstopped ears:

" 'Ye offer polluted bread upon mine altar; and ye say, Wherein have we polluted thee? In that ye say, The table of the Lord is contemptible.' "

Before they had fairly caught their breath after this there came another broadside from the same plain-speaking prophet. It was brought forth by a cloth skirt of good material and not much worn, but so spotted and soiled that Mary Haloran, with one longing look at its texture, had hurled it back into the barrel.

" 'Ye said also, Behold what a weariness is it! and ye have snuffed at it, saith the Lord of hosts; and ye brought that which was torn, and the lame, and the sick; thus ye brought an offering: should I accept this at your hand? saith the Lord.' "

All amusement was now submerged in a rising tide of indignation. The First Church was beginning to realize that it had placed itself in the position of giving a gratuitous insult; which was a shock, for the First Church was well bred, if lacking in missionary zeal. And it was an insult that could not be laid on the narrow shoulders of the Missionary Society. The barrel had been sent from the whole church. That it so poorly represented them they began to see was their own fault.

The enormity of the insult grew with each new disclosure. The packing had been done at a time when closets were being cleared out for the winter, and their surplus contents had been neatly bundled and dumped into the church barrel. From its depths were now brought forth indeed the lame, the halt, and the blind; and with them came texts of Scripture that elucidated the law of sacrifice with startling clearness. It is safe to say that never in the whole reputable life of the First Church had it listened to so pregnant a sermon delivered in so few words. And never, *never* had its understanding been so open to receive with meekness the engrafted word.

" 'And if ye offer the blind for sacrifice, is it not evil?' " sounded the accusing voice; " 'and if ye offer the lame and the sick, is it not evil? Offer it now unto thy governor; will he be pleased with thee, or accept thy person? saith the Lord of hosts.' "

"Why, did you know that all those things were in the Bible?" whispered one astounded woman to another.

"No. But there are a lot of things in the Bible that we never know about till the time comes that we need them. I have found that out. . . . Listen!" For the president was speaking again.

"Ladies, I am glad to say that the text I hold in my hand is the last. I will read it myself. Mrs. Haloran says: "I send this final word from the Mosaic Law, and I beg that the First Church may take it as a message from all its representatives in the mission field, and from Him we serve:

" 'Thou shalt not oppress an hired servant that is poor and needy. . . . At his day thou shalt give him his hire, neither shall the sun go down upon it." Deuteronomy xxiv. 14, 15.

Before Mrs. McArthur had ended the reading the treasurer was on her feet.

"At last, ladies, in my judgment, we have got at the root of the matter. You will find that this minister's salary has not been paid him; now mark my words! And his wife is smarting under a sense of injustice that we should try to supply that deficiency with a barrel of rags."

"Well, I should like to know why it hasn't been paid," said a well-groomed woman, with some severity.

"What do we have a Board for if it isn't to attend to such things?"

"The Board," explained the treasurer with alarming succinctness, "is our agent for disbursing the funds of this church—and others. It cannot honestly pay out what we have not paid in. If you really want to know why this man's salary has not been paid, I will read the delinquent list of this church. Is there a call?"

There was none.

The president tapped. "Ladies, I have not finished the note. Mrs. Haloran continues:

" 'I return the barrel as it was sent, with one exception. In it I found a little half-worn suit with these words pinned to it:' "—a sad-eyed woman in black, who had been listening with strained attention, dropped her face in her hands—" 'It was my little boy's that is gone.' I cried over that little suit. I knew what it cost her to send it. And I accept it as from a sister of the blood. May God bless her and comfort her sad heart.' "

A tearful silence fell upon them then, for, however callous women's hearts may be, there is always one string that vibrates at the thought of the little suit no longer needed.

"Ladies, I have here another letter from Mrs. Haloran, written the next day. She says:

"MY DEAR MADAM:

"After a night of self-abasement I

write to tell you how deeply I regret my action of yesterday and how gladly I would recall it if I could. I cannot yet bring myself to feel that I should have kept the things, but this was an ignoble use to make of the blessed Word of God, and I am filled with sorrow that I should have done it. I will only say in palliation that my husband's salary has been so long overdue—' "

"That's it!" exclaimed the treasurer. "I thought so!"

" '—that we have not been able to spend anything this fall for clothing, for we will not go in debt. We needed everything that is warm, for it is bitter cold out here. You can imagine how like a mockery the barrel seemed to me. We had even used the children's candy money to finish paying the freight.' "

From all over the house came shocked exclamations of "O-h! O-h!" "The children's candy money!" "Shame!"

" 'What I did was against my husband's earnest wishes and entreaties. I know now that he was right and I was wrong; but oh, if the church at home could only be brought to see that what we need is not charity but honest pay!

"Yours for the cause,

"MARY C. HALORAN."

The president laid the letter down.

"Ladies, I never was so humiliated in all my life! That our First Church——"

"Madam President," interrupted an incisive voice, "I should like to know who packed that barrel."

A woman in the second row turned upon her.

"*I* packed that barrel." It was as categorical as question and answer anent Cock Robin. "I am willing to take my share of the blame—*and no more*. I put into that barrel exactly what was sent in, and—as our treasurer has most justly remarked—a disbursing agent can do no more."

"I haven't said that she might not do less," interpolated the treasurer. "If I had been attending to that job

I should have packed most of those things into the furnace—or back to the owners."

All parliamentary procedure was now cast to the winds. They talked when and to whom they pleased.

"I had no right to do anything of the kind," defended the packer. "And I had no reason to assume that you would send me trash to pack."

"That's right, too!" came a voice from the back.

"I will give a word of explanation, Madam President, and then I am through—with this barrel and all others."

"Oh, no!" soothed the president; "you'll pack another one for us some-time and we will do better."

CHRISTMAS BARREL

"Indeed I won't! I am through!
. . . Well, as I say, I left my Christmas work while the rest of you were doing yours, and came down here to pack this barrel—simply because I had promised the president, in a weak moment, that I would do it. I was in a great hurry, and when I saw all these boxes and neat-looking packages I put them in without undoing anything. It was not my business to pass judgment on the things you had sent in." Then in answer to numerous disclaimers: "You didn't send them in? Well, somebody did! Who it was I don't know and *nobody else does*. The sexton doesn't, for I asked him." There was a settling down from strained positions in various parts of the room.

"When I sent off the barrel I considered that my part was done."

"As it certainly was," said the president. "Our thanks are due Mrs. Hall for her work, at any rate. I feel this particularly, since I induced her, much against her will, to undertake it. But the thing that I most deeply deplore, and cannot at all understand, is that this barrel should have been sent out with freight unpaid. We never do that. It is a cardinal point with Missionary Societies that all boxes must be prepaid. I gave my personal check—a blank one to be filled out as was necessary—for this very purpose. That was my contribution."

"And I have just returned it to you," said Mrs. Hall. "It is in that

envelope on the table. The truth of
the matter is that I forgot I had the
check until after the barrel was gone.
Anyway, it seemed to me (being new
to the work as I am) that they ought
to be willing to pay freight on a valu-
able box such as I supposed this was."

"Do you send off your own Christmas gifts that way?" asked the plain-
spoken treasurer.

Mrs. Hall sat down indignantly.

"We'll have to get another treasurer," whispered one missionary worker
to another. "Mrs. Outcault is too
blunt for any use."

"She always hits the nail on the
head, though."

"Yes, but she splits the wood in doing it! I am going to Mrs. Hall's re-

lief. . . . Madam President, I think the lady who did our packing has entirely vindicated herself. We may as well own up to the truth. We were so full of our own selfish concerns that we gave no heed to the call for this missionary barrel in any intelligent way. I, for one, never thought of it once."

The lady who had forgotten to send in the description of the minister's family rose with elaboration.

"I should like to call the lady's attention to the fact that

"Evil is wrought by want of thought
As well as by want of heart."

This sally brought forth a general laugh, which is as good as a barrel of oil for troubled waters.

CHRISTMAS BARREL

"Well, ladies, what will you do with the situation—and the barrel?"

"Madam President,"—a lady was recognized who seldom spoke, but always to the point,—"out of the mouth of this barrel we stand convicted of selfish indifference to a cause we are in duty bound to uphold, and of base desertion of those we have sent to the front and have promised, as Christians, to stand by. I move that we send to this family a box, a real one, that shall be worthy of this church and commensurate with their needs."

There were a dozen seconders.

"I am not sure that they would accept it," suggested the chair.

"Tell them this was intended for a rummage sale," came from the right.

"Or the Salvation Army," from the left.

"Madam President,"—it was the dignified lady whose cheeks had flamed at sight of the opera cloak,—"I feel that I, for one, have been taught a lesson in giving that will last me the rest of my life. I should like to say as much to this brave woman in a note tucked in the pocket of a warm new cloak for herself. I think I can make that acknowledgment so humbly that she will accept the gift."

There was a soft clapping of hands as she sat down.

"That's the right spirit, Madam President," said the lady who had made the motion. "Let us frankly own up to this spirited woman that we see this thing as we never saw it before, and that we are debtors to her for the awakening."

"Madam President,"—this was the donor of one of the vests, who was under an abiding sense of gratitude that nobody knew it,—"I will add to the cloak which Mrs. Caffrey has so generously donated a new overcoat for the minister. I give it as a thank-offering." This lady's husband had recently recovered from a severe illness and this was erroneously taken as a touching allusion to that fact.

The bidding was lively now. The spirit of giving had taken possession of the First Church, and a burning desire to set themselves right. The secretary was kept busy taking down the items, for it was to be no haphazard work this time.

"Madam President,"—it was the treasurer's voice,—"as you know, I don't believe in missionary boxes— they are too often substitutes for the salaries we owe and haven't paid— and I have said that I would never contribute to one; but I've got to put in five pounds of candy for those children if my principles go to smash."

There was loud and prolonged applause from all present.

"Now, ladies," said the chair, when the shower of books, toys, sleds, skates, etc., precipitated by this offer had subsided, "who will volunteer to pack this box? I foresee that it will be quite a task."

CHRISTMAS BARREL

Then up rose the lady who had packed the barrel.

"I'll pack the box. I said I wouldn't, but I will. If Mrs. Outcault's principles have gone to smash, it isn't worth while for me to try to hold on to mine! And—I will pay the freight myself—as a trespass-offering. . . . No, Madam President, I don't want your check."

When the merriment had subsided the treasurer took the floor.

"Madam President and Ladies,—I want to give a word of warning. We will all feel very self-righteous when we go home; and there's danger in it. This box is going to be sent out in a spasm of generosity as the barrel was sent in a spasm of indifference. But let me tell you that *nothing worth living can be supported on spasms!* If any of you see now that the time has come to pay dollars instead of duds, and are willing to live up to your knowledge, hold up your pocketbooks!"

From all over the house went up purses and bags of silver, leather, and filigree.

"Thank the Lord! your conversion is genuine!" cried the treasurer. "But *give me your checks before you go!*"

The beaming president rose.

"You have disposed of the situation beautifully, ladies. But the barrel remains. What shall we do with the barrel?"

"Madam President——"

CHRISTMAS BARREL

"Mrs. Hall."

"We have had our thank-offering, our trespass-offering, and any number of free-will-offerings. I move that we make of the barrel a burnt-offering!"

It was carried by a rising vote amid wild applause.